Grade **3**

KUMON READING WORKBOOKS

Reading

Table of Contents

KUMON

Prefixes

Date   /   /

Name

Level ☆

Score

/100

1 Trace and fill in the words below according to the example.

5 points per question

(1)   up   +   hill   uphill

(2)   down   +   _____   downhill

(3)   in   +   _____   indoors

(4)   out   +   doors   _____

2 Trace or draw lines to match the words to the pictures.

4 points per question

(1)   upstairs   ●

(2)   downstairs   ●

(3)   inside   ●

(4)   outside   ●

(5)   uphill   ●

(6)   downhill   ●

● ⓐ

● ⓑ

● ⓒ

● ⓓ

● ⓔ

● ⓕ

3 Make six words with the puzzle pieces below. Write them in the spaces provided.

24 points for completion

| un | do | use |
| re | tie | usual |

(   )   (   )   (   )

(   )   (   )   (   )

4 Choose the correct words to complete the sentences below.

4 points per question

(1) Look at your shoes! You have to _____ your laces. [retie / unusual]

(2) Your homework had many errors. Please _____ it. [redo / untie]

(3) If you have a key, you can _____ the door. [unlock / untie]

(4) I had to pay for your ice cream. Will you _____ me? [repay / redo]

(5) Why don't you _____ the ribbon on that present and open it?

[untie / retie]

(6) Please _____ your shopping bag. [reuse / redo]

(7) Jane dropped her ice cream. Now she is _____. [unhappy / unfit]

(8) When I got home after vacation, I had to _____. [unpack / repack]

If this was too hard, you can redo the page!

  3

2 Suffixes

Date / /

Name

Level ☆

Score /100

---

1 Trace the words in the example. Then complete the sentences by using the correct form of the word in the box. Add -er or -est as needed.

5 points per question

| fast |

(1) A zebra is a _fast_ runner.

(2) A lion is a _faster_ runner than a zebra.

(3) A cheetah is the _fastest_ of the three.

| high |

(4) The branch on the tree is _____.

(5) The kite is even _____.

(6) The cloud is the _____ of the three.

| young |

(7) Jenna is _____.

(8) Her brother is _____ than she is.

(9) Her baby sister is the _____ in the family.

> ### Don't forget!
>
> An adjective describes a noun. Adding **-er** to the adjective means "more than."
> Adding **-est** means "the most."

---

2 Choose the correct person that matches the description. Write the correct letter in the space provided.

7 points

Patty is taller than her brother.

She is not the tallest of the three children. ( )

A   B   C

---

3 Trace the words in the example. Then complete the sentences with the adjectives from the brackets.

8 points per question

(1) [sunny / sunnier]   Today is ① sunny.

Yesterday was even ② sunnier than today.

(2) [bigger / biggest]   Todd is ①_____ than his sister.

His father is the ②_____ in the family.

(3) [happier / happiest]   I was happy that today was a holiday.

I was even ①_____ when I got the toy I wanted.

I was at my ②_____ when we sang songs.

4 Read the story below. Then answer the questions with words from the story.

8 points per question

The Fair

   Today, Anne is at the fair with her grandpa. He is a farmer, and he grew a big pumpkin. He is hoping to win the prize for the biggest pumpkin at the fair, and Anne also hopes he will win.

   Anne can't believe there are so many awards! There are awards for the best tomato and the sweetest strawberry. She does not understand how they will choose which strawberry is sweetest. What a funny award!

   There are also awards for the prettiest flower and the strangest flower. Some of those flowers are very strange indeed. Anne is sure today will be fun. She can't think of a better way to spend the day.

(1) What prize does Anne's grandpa want to win?

He is hoping to win the prize for the _____.

(2) What does Anne not understand?

Anne does not understand how they will choose which _____

_____.

(3) What is Anne sure about?

Anne is sure today _____.

You are the best!

Suffixes

3

Level ☆

Date / /

Name

Score /100

1 Trace the words to complete the sentences below.

14 points per question

(1) I like to use my pencil. It is very useful when I want to draw.

My scissors are useless when I want to draw.

(2) Sometimes my baby brother needs help. I like to be there so I can be

helpful. It seems that he feels helpless sometimes.

2 Complete the sentences below using the words in the brackets.

4 points per question

(1) [color / colorful]

Art class is fun because we get to use paint. There is so much _____ in

that classroom. It is a very _____ room!

(2) [fear / fearless]

There's no reason to _____ monsters.

They aren't real. Try to be _____ !

(3) [use / useful / useless]

A spoon is a _____ tool! You can _____ it to

stir things, or to pick up things like soup. A spoon is rarely _____.

(4) [help / helpful / helpless]

I like to be _____ around the house. I know my mother can use

my _____. She is not _____, but it's nice for me to be there

for her.

(5) [care / careful / careless]

Knives can be dangerous if you are _____.

You have to take _____ when you hold one.

If you are _____, they are very helpful.

3 Complete the table below.

	adjective	adverb
ex.	sad	sadly
	happy	happily
(1)		neatly
	noisy	(2) noisily
(3)		busily
	hungry	(4)

Don't forget!

An adverb is a word that describes a verb. Adverbs usually have **-ly** endings.
Ex. The girl ate neatly.
When a word ends in **-y**, change the y to **i** and then add **-ly**.
Ex. He hungrily ate the apple.

4 Choose the correct word pair from the box to complete the sentences.

heavy / heavily	light / lightly	happy / happily
quick / quickly	thirsty / thirstily	

(1) My brother is ___happy___. He ___happily___ skips down the street.

(2) The sack of flour is _____. It falls to the ground _____.

(3) The feather is _____. It falls to the ground _____.

(4) That rabbit is _____. It went down into the hole _____.

(5) Jim was _____ after running. He drank water _____.

You did that very quickly!

Compare

4

Date   /   /

Name

1 Draw a line to connect each word below to a word that has a similar meaning.

5 points per question

(1) identical   ●   ● ⓐ hear

(2) quick   ●   ● ⓑ watch

(3) clever   ●   ● ⓒ same

(4) look   ●   ● ⓓ large

(5) listen   ●   ● ⓔ smart

(6) big   ●   ● ⓕ fast

2 Pick a word from the box that is similar to the underlined word in each sentence below. Then write it in the blank.

4 points per question

like	shout	answer	small	last

(1) Tom called to his sister but there was no <u>reply</u>.   (   )

(2) Mrs. Shaver has three <u>little</u> dogs.   (   )

(3) I only <u>enjoy</u> the chewy candies.   (   )

(4) Kim was reading the <u>final</u> chapter of her book.   (   )

(5) Andrew had to <u>yell</u> to stop the bus.   (   )

3 Read the passage. Then put a " ✓ " next to all the phrases that are similar in meaning to the phrase shown in bold below.

30 points for completion

Once there lived an old king. He wasn't interested in the things that interested other kings. He cared only for clothes. He loved clothes. He was never happier than when he was getting new clothes! They were all that he thought about and cared about. The king had a different suit for every hour of the day.

interested in clothes

(   ) (1)   cared for clothes   (   ) (2)   loved clothes

(   ) (3)   thought about clothes   (   ) (4)   had many clothes

(   ) (5)   not like other kings

4 Read the passage. Then copy the underlined words or phrases from the story that mean the same as the words shown below.

5 points per question

If people wanted the king, they could find him with his clothes. He was always busy with his <u>wardrobe</u>. He let his strong <u>knights</u> run his land, even though they were better at fighting than ruling. One day, a pair of <u>tricksters</u> came to the palace. They told the king's fighting men that they were fine <u>tailors</u> and wanted to make the king some new clothes. No one expected them to be playing a joke on the king.

(1)   clothes   (   )

(2)   fighting men   (   )

(3)   people who make clothes   (   )

(4)   people who play jokes   (   )

No one compares to you!

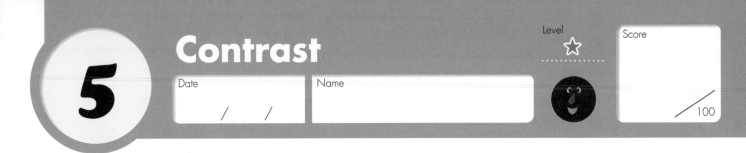

5 Contrast

Level ☆

Date / /

Name

Score

/100

1 Draw a line to match the words below with their opposite.

3 points per question

(1) uphill •

(2) colorful •

(3) quick •

(4) youngest •

(5) happy •

(6) quietly •

• ⓐ oldest

• ⓑ colorless

• ⓒ downhill

• ⓓ slow

• ⓔ unhappy

• ⓕ noisily

2 Circle the word in each sentence below that is the opposite of the word in bold.

4 points per question

(1) Will you continue to study tonight? [**stop**]

(2) Jeff took a cookie from my tray! [**gave**]

(3) Olivia was surprised how tiny her baby sister was. [**huge**]

(4) The puppy destroyed my sandcastle. [**built**]

(5) Lisa's team won all of their games. [**lost**]

(6) Andrew asked me a question. [**answered**]

(7) When Grandpa is angry, he has a funny frown. [**smile**]

(8) Karen was happy when she found her book. [**lost**]

3 Read the story. Then find the underlined word from the story that means the opposite of each word in bold below.

5 points per question

Ella is angry at her little brother. He keeps saying or doing the opposite of what she does. He used to copy her, but now he is doing the opposite. When she turns the light on, he turns the light off. When she says "Good morning!" to the family, he says "Good evening!" with a big smile. It got worse when she built a little house of cards and he destroyed it. She cried, and he laughed. "This has to get better," she said to herself, and then she had an idea.

"If you are so opposite," she said to her brother, "then what should you do when I enter the room?"

"Exit!" said her brother and ran from the room smiling. Now Ella was smiling, too. At last, they were doing the same thing.

(1) **opposite** (same)　　(2) **morning** ( )

(3) **built** ( ) 　　(4) **cried** ( )

(5) **enter** ( )

4 Use a word from the box to complete each sentence below. The word will be the opposite of the word in bold.

5 points per question

worse	disappear	found	sink	arrive

(1) I thought that board game was **lost**. When was it _____?

(2) Jane is sick and trying to get **better**, but she feels _____.

(3) A feather will **float**, but a rock will _____.

(4) Mom always knows when a plane will _____ or **depart**.

(5) Tom can do magic. He can make a coin **appear** or _____!

Did you find the contrasting words?

1 Read the sentences. If both underlined words mean the **same**, circle the "**S**."
If the words are **opposites**, circle the "**O**."

5 points per question

(1) My bag is very <u>heavy</u>. Yours looks <u>light</u>! **S**   **O**

(2) You said that so <u>sadly</u>. Why not say it more <u>cheerfully</u>? **S**   **O**

(3) Sometimes you have to be <u>fearless</u> and <u>brave</u>! **S**   **O**

(4) Jane is using a compass to <u>locate</u> the camp. Can you <u>find</u> it? **S**   **O**

(5) That hat looks like <u>mine</u>. Is it <u>yours</u>? **S**   **O**

(6) Your dog is <u>huge</u>. How did it get so <u>big</u>? **S**   **O**

2 Pick a word from the box that is either the same or the opposite as the word in bold.

5 points per question

cried	fast	first	large	sour	smart

(1) That is one **big** dog! same (   )

(2) My dessert was **sweet**. opposite (   )

(3) We **laughed** for a long time. opposite (   )

(4) That soccer player is really **quick**! same (   )

(5) You got a good grade on your test. You are **clever**! same (   )

(6) I'm reading the **final** chapter of my book. opposite (   )

3 Read the passage. Then complete the chart using words from the passage.

5 points per question

Amy rises early. Cassie wakes up late. Amy goes to bed before nine. Cassie falls asleep after nine. Amy rushes to school. Cassie wastes time on the way to school.

same/compare		different/contrast	
rises	(1) wakes	before	(3)
goes to bed	(2)	rushes	(4)

4 Read the passage. Then complete the chart using words from the passage.

5 points per question

Ducks and swans have some things in common. Both are birds, both can float in the water, and both can fly in the air. A duck is different than a swan, too. A duck is smaller than a swan. A swan is larger than a duck. Most ducks have short necks. A swan usually has a long neck. Ducks can be many colors like white, or yellow, or brown, or green. Swans are usually white.

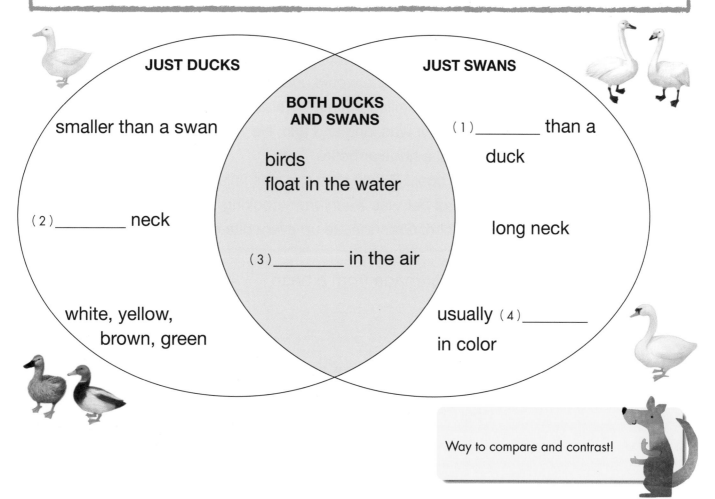

JUST DUCKS

smaller than a swan

(2)_____ neck

white, yellow, brown, green

BOTH DUCKS AND SWANS

birds
float in the water

(3)_____ in the air

JUST SWANS

(1)_____ than a duck

long neck

usually (4)_____ in color

Way to compare and contrast!

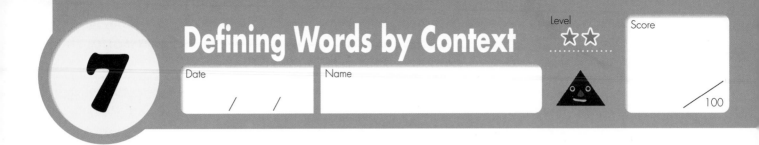

1 Read the first sentence. Then trace or write the word in the definition.

3 points per question

(1) "How tall are you?" I asked. "I am exactly 10 feet in height," said the giant, proudly.

height means how tall someone or something is

(2) Because it was dark, he had to stumble forward blindly.

_____ means to walk in a clumsy way

(3) He kept trying, but he could not solve the difficult math problem.

_____ means to find an answer

2 Read the short passage. Then choose words from the passage to complete the definitions below.

5 points per question

For Grandpa's birthday, Mom said she would cook him anything he wanted. He said he wanted a huge cupcake with vanilla frosting. He also wanted some pasta, and said he liked spaghetti best because it was long and thin. He wanted some pumpkin pie and some garlic bread. He had a huge appetite.

It took Mom a long time to cook! By the time she was finished, even her fingernails were tired. In fact, every part of her was weary from cooking.

The food was great in the end. Grandpa ate up every bite of that large meal.

(1) _____ a flavor made from a bean

(2) _____ hunger

(3) _____ a long, thin type of pasta

(4) _____ thin layers at the tip of each finger

(5) _____ tired

3 Read the sentences below. Then write the word in the box that means the same as the word in bold.

6 points per question

(1) I smiled and was filled with **glee** as I rode down the hill.　[happiness / sorrow]
(　　　　　)

(2) The dancer **twirled** around and around.　[spun / jumped]
(　　　　　)

(3) "I prefer to be called **petite**," said the short woman.　[small / huge]
(　　　　　)

(4) When the flowers **bloom**, our garden will look nice.　[blossom / fall]
(　　　　　)

4 Read the passage. Then trace or draw a line to match the words from the passage to their descriptions below.

7 points per question

"Are you the man sent to help me?" the tall man asked.

"I'm..." I started to answer, but he interrupted me and began talking again.

"As a detective, I need to check for clues," he continued. "I'll need to begin with your fingerprints." He showed me how to push my thumb onto an ink pad and then onto a piece of paper. He looked at my thumb and the piece of paper. The inky purple circles on the paper matched the inky purple circles that were left on my thumb.

"Now I will need to see if they are similar to the man's prints we found," he said.

"Who is he?" I asked.

"I don't know the Mystery Man's name yet," said the detective, "but for your sake, I hope your prints are not the same as the ones we found!"

(1) interrupt　●　　　● ⓐ to keep doing something

(2) detective　●　　　● ⓑ something that is not known

(3) continue　●　　　● ⓒ something that is like something else

(4) fingerprints　●　　　● ⓓ someone who looks for clues

(5) similar　●　　　● ⓔ to start talking before someone else is finished

(6) mystery　●　　　● ⓕ the marks left by the circles on your fingertips

Now you can figure it out!

1 Read the following sentences. Then pick the word from each sentence that completes the definition below.

6 points per question

(1) My brother is small, but he learned karate so that he can defend himself.

_____ is a form of self-defense

(2) Dana had to apologize to her sister for taking her hair clips without asking.

_____ means to say you are sorry

(3) Amit has all sorts of stamps and baseball cards. He likes to collect things.

_____ means to gather similar objects

(4) Grandpa is good with his tools. He built a sturdy doghouse for our dog.

_____ means well-built

2 Read the sentences below. Use the clues in the sentence to choose the correct word from the box to complete each sentence.

6 points per question

subway	barefoot	arrive	nonsense	boring	helmet

(1) Jane doesn't like the _____ because it is underground.

(2) Do you know when the train is supposed to _____?

(3) I don't like wearing shoes. I like going _____!

(4) Don't ride your bike without your _____!

(5) This movie is not interesting. It's long and _____.

(6) Sometimes when she is tired, my sister says things that are _____.

3 Read the passage. Then write the underlined word from the text that matches each definition shown below.

Can you <u>imagine</u> what life must have been like without clocks? It's hard to think of such a different life. What would have happened if someone was <u>curious</u> about the time of day? How would a farmer plan his meal times in the old days? The answer is that life was different. They had to <u>relax</u>, and not worry about the time. Time was just about <u>routine</u> — there was a daily pattern. They would eat breakfast in the morning, lunch when the sun was high in the sky, and dinner around sunset.

(1) not worry ( ) (2) interested in ( )

(3) think of ( ) (4) daily pattern ( )

4 Read the passage. Then write the underlined word from the text that matches each definition shown below.

I'm not sure how I got to this island. I'm not even sure of my name. I don't remember everything, but I remember the storm. A large wave carried me off my ship and <u>overboard</u> into the water.

I could swim well in calm, gentle water, but not the rough and <u>choppy</u> seas of that storm. I was lucky. The waves carried me to a small beach. From there I could drag myself uphill to a wooded <u>thicket</u>.

Those bushes kept me safe until the storm passed. What happened to the <u>wrecked</u> ship, I did not know.

(1) smashed ( )

(2) off a ship and into the water ( )

(3) rough, not calm or gentle ( )

(4) bunch of bushes ( )

You are a dictionary!

1 Complete the chart using words from the passage.

9 points per question

Today, Angela took her first train ride. She went to the train station with her mother and waited on the platform. The heat was almost unbearable. She felt like she might fall down at any moment from being too hot.

The train finally came! It was big and beautiful and loud all at the same time. Angela liked all the steel and steam. She thought that the train was a perfect way to go on a journey. She couldn't wait to travel on such a nice train.

After they found their seats on the train, Angela was looking at the other passengers. How interesting the people were! A man came down the aisle in the middle and took her ticket. He was dressed in a clean uniform.

Angela got out her pillow and got comfortable in her seat. She was ready to go.

Word	Definition
(1) unbearable	something so bad that it is almost impossible to put up with
(2)	people on a train, bus or plane
(3)	an open area between two sections of seats
(4)	the travel between two places
(5)	relaxed

2 Use the puzzle pieces below to create words to finish the sentences.

5 points per question

snow	fire	ering	berg
shiv	ice	ball	place

Brr! These words are about winter!

(1) That _____ you threw was cold and wet!

(2) An _____ is a mountain of ice that floats in the water.

(3) I can't stop _____ because it's so cold out here.

(4) Our family gathers around the _____ when it is cold at night.

3 Unscramble the words below to finish the sentences.

5 points per question

(1) Your father called from the _____ to say he'll be late.   [ice / off]

(2) The _____ made a big feast for the town.   [ef / ch]

(3) I really like my eggs _____ in the morning.   [ed / am / scr / bl]

(4) We will _____ your birthday tomorrow!   [e / brate / cel]

(5) I like to kick the _____ ball around.   [cc / so / er]

(6) In many Asian countries, people eat with _____.
                                                          [op / sti / ch / cks]

(7) We _____ behind the table to surprise her.   [ed / ch / crou]

Way to unscramble!

10

Defining Words by Context

Level

Date   /   /

Name

Score

/100

1 Complete the passage using the vocabulary words defined below.   6 points per question

Today when I got home, I ran inside. I was (1) _____ all day at school. I couldn't stop thinking about a program on television that I wanted to watch. It was about space travel. I wanted to be an (2) _____ and go into space. It would be so much fun to walk in space! I really wanted to (3) _____ new places, and space seemed like a really big new place!

> **astronaut**: a person who travels into space
>
> **explore**: to travel and study new places
>
> **excited**: to get so happy it is difficult to relax

2 Read the following sentences. Then pick the word from each sentence that completes the definition below.   7 points per question

(1) Our dog is very clever. He always knows the right time to beg for food.

_____ means smart or mentally quick

(2) The two coats were identical. I couldn't tell them apart.

_____ means the same

(3) I am very careful to stay on the sidewalk when I walk to school.

_____ means a paved walk on the side of the road

(4) Jane wants to be an explorer. She wants to go on an adventure in a new land.

_____ means a journey involving risk and danger

3 Unscramble the words below to finish the sentences.

4 points per question

(1) All _____ go into space.   [as / nauts / tro]

(2) A monkey _____ from the zoo.   [ed / es / cap]

(3) Last night I dreamed that I was on an _____ in a new world!

[ven / ad / ture]

(4) I can't get _____ in this seat.   [for / com / ble / ta]

(5) Remember to stay on the _____ !   [si / wa / de / lk]

(6) There aren't many _____ on this bus.   [pa / en / ss / gers]

4 Read the sentences below. Use the clues in the sentence to choose the correct word from the box to complete each sentence.

5 points per question

station	explored	identical	clever	excited	chased

(1) Columbus _____ many different new lands.

(2) The twins are _____, and nobody can tell them apart.

(3) Our _____ cat figured out how to open the bag of food.

(4) I waited at the train _____ for hours.

(5) I _____ the mouse out of our house.

(6) I am very _____ about my birthday party today.

Good job!

Level ★★

Score / 100

1 Make ten words by connecting the balloons below. You may reuse a balloon to make a new word.

60 points for completion

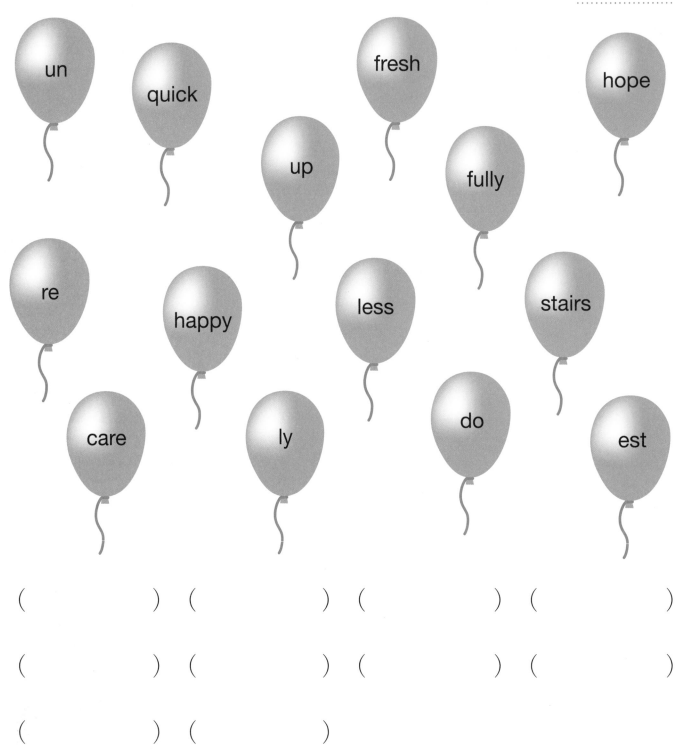

( ) ( ) ( ) ( )

( ) ( ) ( ) ( )

( ) ( )

2 Complete the crossword puzzle using the sentences below as clues. Use capital letters.

5 points per question

(6)
(7)
(1) C R U
H
P
(5)
(8)
(2) F O L
(3) O C E
M
G
(4) I G N
T
L
L
E

ACROSS

(1) My parents are always __?__ about my grades.

(2) Baseball is okay, but I always look forward to __?__ in the fall.

(3) Can you __?__ the correct place for this word?

(4) I can't __?__ how happy you must have been when you won!

DOWN

(5) Mrs. Will can't find the __?__. She only has the copy.

(6) When you get lost in a forest, a __?__ is a useful tool.

(7) My dog gets very tired when we walk __?__.

(8) It's a long ride, so make sure you get __?__.

You're a star!

12

Who / What / When / Where
Two Types of People

Level

Date / /

Name

Score
/ 100

1 Read the passage. Then answer the questions using words from the passage.

10 points per question

Angela is an early bird. Her brother Samson is a night owl.

Samson likes to stay up all night reading comics. He also plays video games. He likes it when the house is dark and quiet. He seems to like it when there is nobody around. Angela likes to be around people.

Angela rises at dawn to do her chores. She cleans her room every day before getting ready for school. She likes reading books in the kitchen in the morning light. Everything seems bright and sunny in the morning. The cat is also very playful early in the day, and Angela likes the cat.

Samson doesn't like cats. He never cleans his room. He hates mornings.

(1) Who likes the night more?

_____ likes the night more.

(2) What does Samson do at night?

Samson reads _____ and plays _____ all night.

(3) When does Angela rise to do her chores?

Angela _____ to do her chores.

(4) Where does Angela like to read?

Angela likes to read books in the _____ in the _____.

(5) When do the two children clean their rooms?

Angela cleans her room _____ before _____

_____.

Samson _____.

2 Read the passage. Then answer the questions below.

Angela and Samson are different in other ways, too. Sometimes Angela is surprised that they are brother and sister.

Angela is grumpy at night. Samson is grumpy in the morning. Angela has a big breakfast and a small dinner. Samson sometimes has no breakfast! For dinner, he usually has as much as he can eat.

Angela likes to plan her day. Her homework is always organized. Samson never plans his day, and he is always late in the morning. He often forgets when his tests are. Angela is always ready for a test.

Samson does not care. He knows that they are different, but he loves his sister. He also knows that she will help him study. Angela knows that Samson will teach her how to play video games if she asks. Yes, they are still brother and sister, even if they are very different.

(1) Underline the word in the passage that answers this question:　　　　10 points

What is Angela's homework always like?

(2) Answer the questions below using text from the passage.　　　10 points per question

① When is Samson grumpy?

Samson is grumpy _____.

② Who is always ready for a test?

_____ is always ready for a test.

③ What does Samson know his sister will do?

Samson knows his sister will _____.

④ What will Samson teach his sister if she asks?

Samson will teach his sister how to _____
if she asks.

Which person are you like, Angela or Samson?

Who / What / When / Where
Sleeping Animals

13

Level ★★

Date / /

Name

Score /100

1 Read the passage. Then answer the questions using words from the passage.

10 points per question

> Sleep is a very important part of our lives. After a long day, we all like that feeling of a soft blanket and pillow. We know how good it will feel in the morning after we get some rest. Did you know that sleep is also important to animals? They also have to sleep after they work hard.
>
> Some animals sleep in the sea. Fish have no eyelids, so they sleep with their eyes open! Sea otters sleep in seaweed on the top of the sea. The seaweed keeps the otters from drifting. Most sharks have to keep swimming while they sleep, but they still have to sleep! Some fish find a little hole in the coral and hide so they can sleep. The clown fish turns on his side at the bottom of the sea in order to sleep. That sounds like what people do!

(1) What feeling do we all like?

We all like that feeling of _____.

(2) When do animals have to sleep?

They have to sleep after _____.

(3) Where do sea otters sleep?

Sea otters sleep in _____ on the _____.

(4) Who has to keep swimming while they sleep?

Most _____ have to keep _____ while they sleep.

(5) Which animal in the sea sleeps the most like people do?

The _____ sleeps the most like people do.

2 Read the passage. Then answer the questions using words from the passage.

Some animals sleep under the ground! When it's hot, many frogs sleep in a hole because they want to escape the heat. Some frogs will spend an entire summer in their hole. Groundhogs live in holes in the ground, so they also sleep underground. They make tunnels with two openings. Foxes can take a groundhog's home, and then use it as their own home. The fox will sleep in the groundhog's bed!

What about the animals that live above the ground? Birds will sleep in their nests or on branches. Did you know that a bird's claws close when they fall asleep? This helps them stay on the branch. Bats sleep upside down. They also sleep 20 hours a day! Bats are the champions of sleeping. One kind of smart lizard sleeps all the way out on a leaf at the end of a branch. If a snake tries to come eat it, the branch will move and the lizard will drop. Amazing!

No matter what kind of animal you are, you need your sleep.

(1) Who sleeps in a hole during the summer?

Many _____ sleep in a hole during the summer.

(2) What kind of tunnels do groundhogs make?

Groundhogs make tunnels with _____.

(3) What animal can take a groundhog's home?

_____ can take a groundhog's home.

(4) When do a bird's claws close?

A bird's claws close when they _____.

(5) Where does one kind of smart lizard sleep?

One kind of smart lizard sleeps all the way out on a _____ at the end of a _____.

I like to sleep too!

Who / What / When / Where
The Cheetah / The Contest

14

Level ★★

Score /100

Date / /

Name

1 Read the passage. Then answer the questions using words from the passage.

8 points per question

> The cheetah is the fastest animal in the world. It can run faster than a person on a bike! In order to run so fast, cheetahs have large noses, which help them breathe easier, and strong hearts. They can't run fast for very long. Once they stop, they have to rest before they can go on.
>
> Cheetahs are large cats with brown spots all over their yellow fur. These spots make it hard for other animals to see them in the tall yellow grass in Africa. They are very good at hunting and are dangerous.
>
> The word 'cheetah' comes from an Indian word meaning "spotted one," but there have been no wild cheetahs in India since about 1940.
>
> Some kings and rulers had cheetahs as pets in ancient times, but now they are very rare animals in the wild and are protected.

(1) Why do cheetahs have big noses and strong hearts?

Cheetahs have big noses and strong hearts so they can _____.

(2) What color are the spots on a cheetah?

The cheetah has _____.

(3) Since when have there been no wild cheetahs in India?

There have been no wild cheetahs in India since about _____.

(4) Where do cheetahs hunt?

Cheetahs hunt in the tall yellow _____ in Africa.

(5) In ancient times, who had cheetahs as pets?

In ancient times, some _____ had cheetahs as pets.

2 Read the passage. Then answer the questions using words from the passage.

20 points per question

Once, an old ruler of China held a contest. He gave out seeds to each child. "Who wants to be the next emperor?" he asked, smiling. "The young man who can show the best results next year will become the next emperor!"

Young Jun loved to grow flowers. He was very happy to see what his seed would do. Jun had grown many beautiful plants. These seeds, however, did not grow. He tried using bigger pots. He tried using better soils. Still, nothing grew. As the other boys' plants grew taller and taller, he grew sadder and sadder.

At last, Young Jun had to go see the old ruler. He carried his empty pot with him.

When the old ruler saw him, he asked, "Why did you bring me an empty pot?" "I did my best," cried Jun. "No matter what I did, this seed would not grow."

The old ruler smiled. "This empty pot is worth more to me than all the other flowers in the land. This empty pot holds only the truth. None of the seeds could grow. Only this boy was brave enough to see the truth. He shall be the next ruler of all China."

(1) Who did the old emperor need to find?

The old emperor needed to find the _____ who could be

the _____.

(2) Why did Jun grow sadder?

He grew sadder because _____

_____, while nothing grew in his pot.

(3) Why did the emperor say that Jun's empty pot was worth more to him than all the other flowers in the land?

He said that because only Jun was _____ to show an empty

pot that held _____.

The truth is always the best way to go!

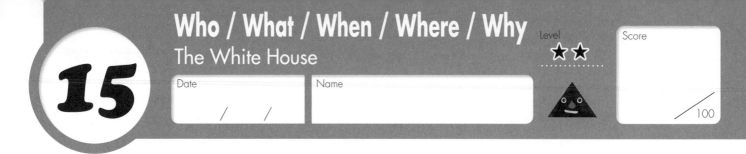

15

Who / What / When / Where / Why
The White House

Level ★★

Date / /

Name

Score /100

1 Read the passage. Then answer the questions using words from the passage.

10 points per question

> For over 200 years, the White House has been the home of the American president and his family. In 1790, George Washington chose where the White House would be built. But he never lived there. In fact, George Washington is the only president who never lived in the White House. The house was not finished until 1800.
>
> In 1800, the new president, John Adams, and his wife moved into the White House, and ever since, the president and his family have lived in the White House.

(1) Who lives in the White House?

The White House is the home of the American _____ and

_____.

(2) What did George Washington do in 1790?

In 1790, George Washington chose where the _____

would be _____.

(3) Who was the only president who never lived in the White House?

_____ was the only president who never lived in

the White House.

(4) Why did George Washington never live in the White House?

The house _____ until 1800.

(5) Who moved into the White House in 1800?

In 1800, the new president, _____, and his wife moved in.

2 Read the passage. Then answer the questions using words from the passage.

10 points per question

The first White House did not last long. During the War of 1812, the White House was burned down. After the war, all 62 rooms of the White House were built again.

Later, the house was expanded for the first time and office space was added. That area is called the West Wing now. Harry Truman added more rooms and space in 1948.

Now the White House is very large. It has 132 rooms and 35 bathrooms. There are 412 doors, 147 windows and 28 fireplaces! The White House kitchen can feed up to 140 for dinner. There are six levels to the White House, too.

(1) What happened to the White House during the War of 1812?

The White House was _____ during the War of 1812.

(2) How was the White House expanded for the first time?

_____ was added when the White House was expanded for the first time.

(3) Where is the office space in the White House?

The office space is in the area called the _____.

(4) Who added more rooms in 1948?

President _____ added more rooms and space in 1948.

(5) How many people can the White House kitchen feed?

The White House kitchen can feed up to _____ people.

Have you visited the White House?

Who / What / When / Where / Why / How

A Purple Gift

16

Date / /

Name

Level ★★

Score / 100

1 Read the passage. Then answer the questions below.

Ben was hoping for a video game for his birthday. There was also a board game he was thinking about. At the very least, he was sure he could get some comics.

He did get some comics, and he did get the board game. But the very last package? It was from his sister Karen. He slowly unwrapped the package. It didn't feel like a video game.

It was a purple sweater. Purple was his least favorite color. He smiled and thanked Karen nicely, but he never wanted to wear that sweater. He couldn't wear purple!

He quickly put the sweater away in his bottom drawer. Then he ran off to play his new board game with his family.

(1) Underline the word in the passage that answers this question:
Who gave Ben his very last present of the day?

10 points

(2) Answer the questions below using text from the passage.

10 points per question

① What was the very last present?

The very last present was a _____.

② When did Ben want to wear the sweater?

Ben _____.

③ Why did Ben not want to wear it?

Ben didn't want to wear it because he couldn't _____.

④ How did Ben put the present away?

Ben _____ put the sweater away.

2 Read the passage. Based on the answers to the questions below, fill in the blanks with the correct underlined words.

10 points per question

One day a few weeks later, Ben's mother asked him about the sweater.

"Why don't you wear your sister's sweater today?" she asked one day. "She made it just for you!"

"I am not cold," he said without thinking. That day he was (1) _____ all day.

Then one night they were going to dinner as a family. His (2) _____ asked him to wear the sweater again. "I don't want to wear it because I hate it," he (3) _____ replied.

"Ben," said his mother, "I know it's not the nicest sweater in the world, but think about how important Karen is to you. You know she will be (4) _____ if you wear it just this once."

Ben walked (5) _____ to his room. He knew she was right. He wore the sweater to dinner. His sister smiled all night.

ⓐ   Who asked Ben to wear his sister's sweater to dinner?
Ben's <u>mother</u> asked him to wear his sister's sweater to dinner.

ⓑ   How did Ben reply when his mother asked him to wear the sweater to dinner?
Ben replied <u>hastily</u> when his mother asked him to wear the sweater to dinner.

ⓒ   What happened when Ben didn't wear the sweater?
Ben was <u>cold</u> all day.

ⓓ   How would his sister feel if he wore the sweater to dinner?
His sister would be <u>proud</u> if he wore it just once.

ⓔ   How did Ben walk to his room?
Ben walked <u>slowly</u> to his room.

You did that swiftly!

© Kumon Publishing Co., Ltd.   33

Vocabulary Review

Level ★★

1 Choose the correct word from the box to complete the sentences below.

5 points per question

| crouched | expanded | cheetah | rare | beautiful | results |

(1) The balloon _____ when we put more air in it.

(2) Gorillas are _____ animals. There aren't many of them.

(3) The _____ is the fastest animal on four legs!

(4) We _____ behind the bushes to scare my sister.

(5) When I try my best, the _____ are almost always good.

(6) Roses are _____ flowers.

2 Write the letters to complete the words below.

5 points per question

(1) My b l _ _ _ _ _ t fell off my bed last night.

(2) Your favorite s w _ _ t _ _ has a hole in it!

(3) The p r _ _ _ d _ _ t has to make a lot of speeches.

(4) Mother has to spend a lot of time at her o f _ _ c _.

(5) Cheetahs are very d a _ _ _ _ r _ _ _ animals. They are fast, and have sharp teeth!

(6) Our team won all of the games. We were the c h _ _ p _ _ _ _!

3 Complete the crossword puzzle using the sentences below as clues. Use capital letters.

5 points per question

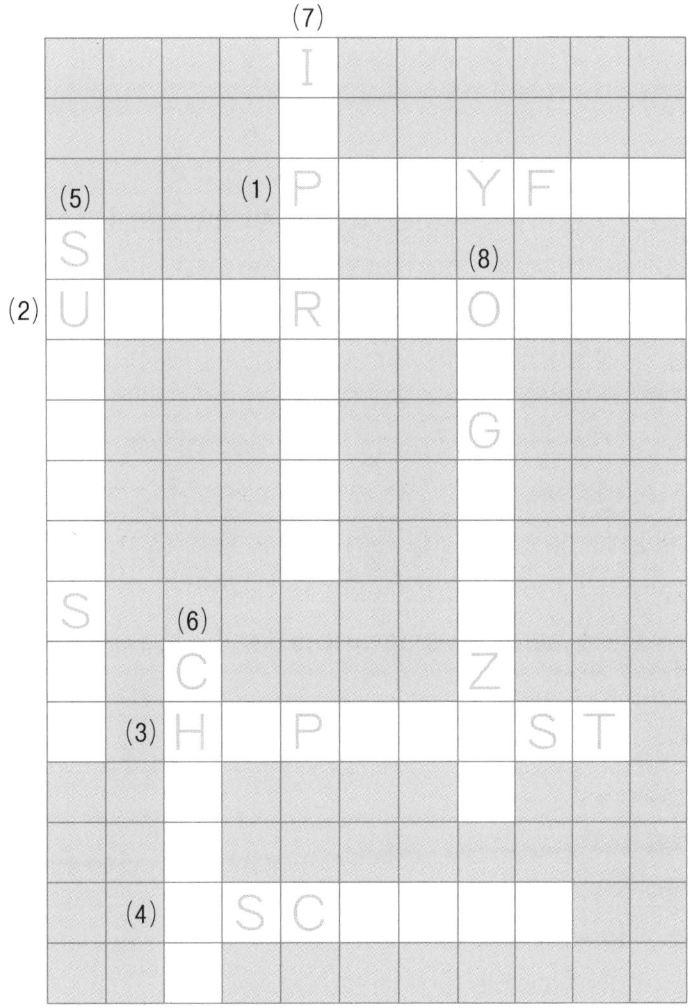

(Crossword grid)

(7) I

(5) (1) P   Y F

S   (8)

(2) U   R   O

G

S   (6)

C   Z

(3) H   P   S T

(4) S C

ACROSS

(1) My cat is very ___?___. She loves to play with string!

(2) Groundhogs live ___?___ in holes.

(3) Grace is at her ___?___ when she is reading a book in the sun.

(4) I have no idea how our hamster ___?___ from his cage.

DOWN

(5) Drew will be very ___?___ when we jump out from behind his bed.

(6) I get my pocket money if I finish all my ___?___.

(7) Trying your hardest in school is very ___?___.

(8) My mom is always telling me that I am messy and need to be more ___?___.

Good job!

Chart the Passage
Caroline's Soup

18

Level ★★

Date / /

Name

Score /100

1 The following passages need titles. Look at the chart for each passage, and then write the correct title in the blank provided.

23 points per question

Caroline saw that her mother was tired.

"Mom, may I help you make dinner tonight?"

"Of course you may," her mother said. "How nice of you to offer! First, we have to make a list of all the things we need. We will go shopping for the vegetables at the grocery store. We will also need to buy fish at the fish store. Then we need to bring it all home and start cooking! Do you still want to help?"

"Yes, mom, that's not so bad! Let's go shopping!" Caroline replied.

---

(1)

Title:
i. make a shopping list
ii. get vegetables at the grocery store
iii. get fish at the fish store

Possible titles: ⓐ Caroline's Wish List

ⓑ Mom Is Going to the Store

ⓒ How to Get Ready to Cook Dinner

At the grocery store they bought lots of vegetables. They found the carrots and the corn. They bought potatoes and tomatoes. They were going to make soup! They needed all sorts of vegetables. They also needed fruit for dessert, so they got strawberries and blueberries. Ice cream was important, too. The fruit was going to taste really good on top of the ice cream. Caroline pushed the cart while her mother shopped. It was fun.

---

(2)

Title:
i. vegetables
ii. fruit
iii. ice cream

Possible titles: ⓐ Things They Got at the Grocery Store

ⓑ Things to Go in the Soup

ⓒ Things that Caroline Wanted

2 Complete the chart below with information from the passage.

6 points per question

Finally it was time to make dinner!

To make the soup, they first put in the onions, and then water. Then came the carrots, garlic, and potatoes. Last, they put in the fish and some salt and pepper, and then they let it boil. Now it was time to make the salad. The salad had bell peppers, tomatoes, and spinach in it. Caroline chose the dressing.

Then it was time to get the dessert ready. They put a little sugar in some water and cooked the berries. The strawberries and blueberries made the sauce red and blue. The sauce was going to be great on their ice cream!

Caroline was very hungry by the time the dinner was ready. She was glad she helped her mother cook dinner.

Dish	Ingredients (What goes in the dish)
Soup	(1) _____, water (2) _____, garlic, potatoes salt and (3) _____, and (4) _____
(5) _____	(6) _____ peppers, tomatoes, (7) _____ dressing
Dessert	(8) _____, blueberries, (9) _____ and water, ice cream

Way to chart that passage!

Chart the Passage
Time and the Seasons

19

Level ★★

Date / /

Name

Score

/100

1 The following passages need titles. Look at the chart for each passage, and then write the correct title in the blank provided. 30 points per question

Long ago, most people did not have or use clocks. Instead, they looked at the sun and the moon. Was the sun out? Was it sunset? Was the moon full? They ate according to the sun, and slept when the moon was out. As the seasons changed, so did their activities. Only a few people divided their time more exactly. During the day these people used a sundial. At night, they watched how the stars moved.

(1)

Title:
i. rising and setting of the sun
ii. phases of the moon
iii. changing of the seasons

Possible titles: ⓐ How People Planned Their Days Long Ago
ⓑ Parts of the Solar System
ⓒ How to Use a Sundial At Night

Some people marked hours and minutes by using a sundial. The most common sundial was a large horizontal circle with a rod pointing up. The rod made a shadow on the circle. That shadow worked like the small hand on a modern clock. As the sun moved across the sky, the shadow moved around the circle like the small hand on a clock or watch.

(2)

Title:
i. large horizontal circle
ii. small rod pointing up
iii. rod creates shadow in sun
iii. as sun moves, shadow moves around the circle

Possible titles: ⓐ Daytime Chores
ⓑ Shadows of Time
ⓒ How a Sundial Works

2 Complete the chart below with information from the passage. Make sure all the verb tenses agree.

4 points per question

Farmers' chores have always been based on the seasons rather than the time on a watch. In the North, spring was a time for plowing and planting. First farmers planted oats, then corn, and then their other vegetables. Summer was the time to pull weeds and mow hay. They would gather, or harvest, the wheat and the other grains they had planted the fall before. Shade was provided for the animals so they wouldn't get too hot. Fall was for picking apples and planting grain. Winter was the time to stock up on firewood, and to spin and weave cloth.

Season	Chores Done
Spring	(1) _____, planting (2) _____, corn, and other vegetables
Summer	pulling (3) _____, mowing the (4) _____, harvesting the wheat and other (5) _____ providing (6) _____ for the animals
Fall	(7) _____ apples, (8) _____ grain
Winter	stocking up on (9) _____, spinning and (10) _____ cloth

Way to chart that passage!

Chart the Passage
Ski Vacation

Level ★★

Date / /

Name

Score

/100

---

1 Read the following passage. Then answer the questions below.

30 points per question

> Toby's family was going on a ski vacation! Toby thought it was going to be so much fun. He couldn't wait. The snow was going to be cold and wet, and the sun was going to be warm. He loved the feeling of skiing down a mountain. The vacation was going to be great.
>
> The only bad thing about going to ski was all the equipment! There was so much stuff. You had to bring skis and ski boots, of course. You also had to wear big socks to keep your feet warm, and long underwear for your legs. And you couldn't forget your hat and mittens, or you would freeze.

Hiking a Mountain	Why a Ski Vacation Was Going to Be Fun
Ski Equipment	Scary Ski Vacation

(1) Pick a good title for the first paragraph from the box above.

Title:
i. snow was going to be cold and wet
ii. sun was going to be warm
iii. the feeling of skiing down the mountain

(2) Pick a good title for the second paragraph from the box above.

Title:
i. skis and ski boots
ii. socks and long underwear
iii. hat and mittens

2 Complete the charts below with information from the passage. Make sure all the verb tenses agree.

> One thing Toby never liked was getting a ski lesson. He knew he had some more to learn, but he did not like the teachers. They always made silly jokes when Toby just wanted to ski. The lessons always took very long because they had to wait for everyone to get ready. Every year, someone always cried. That also made lessons bad.
>
>
>
> This year, though, he was glad to have the instructors. The teachers were actually very helpful. When his hat flew off while he was going down the mountain, they went and got it for him. They pointed out how he could stop faster. They helped him figure out how to make turns better. Lessons were not so bad after all!

(1) Complete this chart for the first paragraph.

10 points per question

Why Toby Didn't Like Lessons
He did not like the teachers.
Lessons always took ①_____.
Someone always ②_____.

(2) Complete this chart for the second paragraph.

10 points per question

Why Toby Changed His Mind About Lessons
The teachers got his hat for him when he lost it.
The teachers pointed out how he could ①_____.
They helped him figure out how to make ②_____.

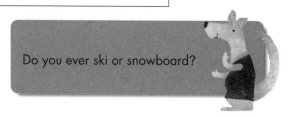

Do you ever ski or snowboard?

Chart the Passage
Did You Know?

21

Level ★★

Date / /

Name

Score /100

1 Complete the chart with information from the passage.

5 points per question

> Of all the rivers in the world, the Nile is the longest. It travels 4,157 miles north from the Sudan to Egypt. The Mississippi is the third-longest river, stretching 3,471 miles through the center of the U.S.A. The Amazon, located mostly in the country of Brazil, weaves through the rainforest for 4,082 miles.

RIVER	LOCATION	LENGTH
The (1) _____	from the Sudan to Egypt	4,157 miles
The Amazon	mostly in (2) _____	(3)
The Mississippi	center of the (4) _____	3,471 miles

2 Complete the chart with information from the passage.

5 points per question

> Many people once believed that nature was controlled by gods. The Greeks and Romans called the same gods by different names. When the Greeks went out to sea, they looked to Poseidon for help. In Rome, that same god was called Neptune. The Greek messenger of the gods was Hermes. The Romans called him Mercury. The god Cupid, the Roman god of love, was called Eros in Greece. He was thought to bring love to the world.

GREEK NAME	ROMAN (1) _____	RESPONSIBILITY
(2)	Neptune	ruler of the seas
Hermes	Mercury	(3)
Eros	(4)	god of love

3

Read the following passage. Then answer the questions below.

20 points per question

The two biggest planets in our solar system are Jupiter and Saturn. You can see Jupiter from Earth at night. It is the largest planet in our solar system, and it is mostly made of gas. Jupiter is also an interesting planet — it has over sixty-three moons. The easiest way to tell Jupiter apart from the other planets is its red spot. The big red spot is actually a storm! Jupiter is the fifth planet from the sun.

Saturn is the sixth planet from the sun and also has a very unusual look. It has rings around it. The rings are made of ice and dust. Saturn also has many moons. Sixty-one moons orbit the planet, which is also made mostly of gas.

(1) Fill this chart out for Jupiter.

Number Planet From the Sun	Number of Moons	Unusual Mark
① The _____ planet from the sun	②	③ red spot

(2) Fill this chart out for Saturn.

Number Planet From the Sun	Number of Moons	Unusual Mark
① The _____ planet from the sun	②	③

(3) What would be the best choice for a title for this passage? Put a check (✓) next to the best title.

( ) ⓐ Saturn and Jupiter: The Two Biggest Planets

( ) ⓑ Saturn and Jupiter in Space

( ) ⓒ Saturn and Jupiter Together at Last

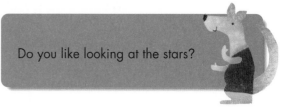

Do you like looking at the stars?

Chart the Passage

Birds, Birds, Birds!

22

Date / /

Name

1 Read the following passage. Then answer the questions below.

You don't have to go far to see some interesting birds. Many of them will show up right in your backyard! Cardinals and sparrows may already be there in your bushes looking for food. Male cardinals are red and eat seeds. Sparrows are brown and eat seeds too. Both sparrows and cardinals sing beautiful songs. A robin might show up in your backyard hunting for worms. Robins have a rust-colored chest. If you put up a birdfeeder in your backyard, you might attract blue jays and woodpeckers! Blue jays are mainly blue and will eat many things, including acorns. Woodpeckers also eat many different things, but they mostly eat insects. They can be any color, too! Next time you want to see a bird, try your backyard.

(1) Complete the chart with information from the passage.   5 points per question

Type of Bird	Main Color	Food
Male Cardinal	red	①
②	brown	seeds
Robin	rust	③
Blue Jay	④	acorns
⑤	any	⑥

(2) Put a check (✓) next to the best title for the passage.   10 points

( ) ⓐ How to Hunt Birds

( ) ⓑ Blue Jays Will Eat Anything

( ) ⓒ Interesting Birds Right in Your Own Backyard

2 Read the following passage. Then answer the questions below.

Of course, if you have too many birds in your backyard, you may start getting some uninvited guests. There are birds that hunt other birds, too. They are called birds of prey. Hawks are (1) _____ birds and can see from far away. They also have sharp beaks and sharp talons, or claws, on their feet. They can be scary! Eagles hunt during the (2) _____ like hawks, and are the (3) _____ birds in this group of birds of prey. Did you know that owls also hunt other birds? Most (4) _____ are smaller than these other two birds, and they hunt at (5) _____.

Each bird has its own kind of home. Hawks make nests in any kind of tree, and even utility (6) _____ on the side of highways. Eagles prefer tall trees or (7) _____ for their nests. Owls don't bother with building their own nests. They just find good spots in (8) _____, caves, or even other birds' old nests.

(1) Complete the passage with information from the chart.   5 points per question

Type of Bird	Hunting Time	Size	Nest
Hawk	day	big	trees and poles
Eagle	day	biggest	trees and cliffs
Owl	night	smallest	barns, caves and old nests

(2) Put a check (✓) next to the best title for the passage.   20 points

(   ) ⓐ Birds that Hunt

(   ) ⓑ Backyard Birds

(   ) ⓒ Birds in the Sky

You've got eyes like a hawk!

Chart the Passage
Who Did It?

Level
★★

Date / /

Name

Score
/100

1 Read the following passage. Then answer the questions below.

Someone ate Kim's pizza! Kim left some pizza in the kitchen, and when she came back, it was gone. She decided to interview everyone and ask them what they ate for lunch. That way she would find the person who ate her pizza!

First, she asked her dad.

"Hmm, well I didn't have a sandwich, and I didn't have spaghetti, but I forget what I actually had! Maybe it was the soup."

"You're no help at all!" Kim said, and went to find her mom.

"What did I have? Well, I didn't have the soup, or a sandwich. I can't remember what I did have, though!"

"Why can't anyone remember?" Kim said. Only three people had lunch, and Kim was starving. She could not find her brother to ask him. When she went to the kitchen, she could see that one person had a sandwich, one person had soup, and one person ate the pizza. Who had the pizza?

(1) Complete the chart with information from the passage.   10 points per question

Person	Lunch
Dad	①
Mom	②
Brother	③

(2) What is the best title for this passage? Put a check (✓) next to the best title.

20 points

( ) ⓐ The Family That Can't Remember

( ) ⓑ Lunch for Sale

( ) ⓒ The Case of the Stolen Pizza

2 Complete the passage with information from the chart.

10 points per question

After she figured out that her mom had eaten her pizza, Kim was angry. Her father made her some spaghetti to make her feel better, but it wasn't working. Then, when she went up to her room, she saw that her favorite jacket was gone!

"Who took my jacket?" she shouted from her room. It looked like she was going to have to investigate some more. This time, she found her brother, and he was playing (1) _____.

"What were you doing earlier?" she asked him.

"Uhhh, I guess I was reading my (2) _____," he said.

Her mother was no better. She was fixing her bike, and had fixed (3) _____ before that. Her mother was very confused as Kim stomped off.

"Dad, what were you doing earlier?" Kim asked her father, who was (4) _____ on the sofa.

"Silly girl, I made you some (5) _____! What is this about?" he answered.

"I can't find my jacket!" Kim blurted out.

"Oh! I took that to the cleaners yesterday because it was dirty!" said her father. Kim felt better. She had solved another case.

Person	What They Were Doing When Kim Asked	What They Were Doing Earlier
Mom	fixing her bike	fixing Kim's bike
Dad	reading on the sofa	making spaghetti
Brother	playing video games	reading comic books

You figured it out!

47

24

Sequencing
My Birthday Party

Date / /

Name

Level ★★★

Score /100

1 Read the title of the story. Then put the correct number under each picture so that the story is in the correct order.

45 points for completion

Baking a Cake for My Birthday

(1)

( ) Then I waited for an hour.

(2)

( ) Then I put the batter in the pan.

(3)

(1) First, I got all the ingredients out.

(4)

( ) Then I put the ingredients in a bowl.

(5)

( ) Yum! This cake is good!

(6)

( ) I mixed the batter.

(7)

( ) I put the pan in the oven.

(8)

( ) I buttered the pan before putting the batter in it.

(9)

( ) Then I waited for the cake to cool.

2 Read the passage and answer the questions below.

Baking the cake was the last thing that went well during my birthday party. My first friends arrived while we were still cleaning up the mess in the kitchen. When we moved the cake to the backyard, we dropped it in the grass! We saved some of the cake, but not much.

Then, when we got back to the kitchen, we saw that we left the ice cream out the whole time. It was completely melted! One boy fell and skinned his knee by the pool. Then it started raining. When we went inside to watch movies, the television broke. What a day! At least I liked the gifts I got at the end.

(1) Number the sentences to match the order they occur in the passage.

40 points for completion

(   ) ⓐ I got gifts that I liked.

(   ) ⓑ A boy skinned his knee by the pool.

(   ) ⓒ The television broke.

(   ) ⓓ The ice cream melted.

(   ) ⓔ My friends arrived while we were still cleaning up.

(   ) ⓕ We dropped the cake in the backyard.

(   ) ⓖ It started raining.

(   ) ⓗ We baked a cake.

(2) What is a good title for this passage? Put a check (✓) next to the best title.

15 points

(   ) ⓐ The Perfect Birthday Party

(   ) ⓑ The Case of the Melted Ice Cream

(   ) ⓒ The Birthday Party Where Everything Went Wrong

A bad birthday party is still a birthday party!

Making Predictions
Little Thunder and the Fawn

Level ★★★

Date / /

Name

Score /100

1 Read the passage and answer the questions below.

30 points per question

> A long time ago, Little Thunder was a member of a large tribe. This quiet tribe tried not to disturb the world around them, and they hunted animals only when needed for food or clothes. Once, when the tribe was very hungry, Little Thunder went hunting. He came to a forest clearing and he saw grass move. He dropped to the ground and waited. He tested the direction of the breeze by wetting a finger in his mouth and holding it in the air. His finger felt cool, and he knew the wind was blowing toward him. Whatever was in the grass would not catch his scent. He was sure the animal would not smell him.

(1) Number the sentences to match the order they occur in the passage.

( ) ⓐ Little Thunder held his finger in the air.

( ) ⓑ Little Thunder wet his finger in his mouth.

( ) ⓒ Little Thunder saw grass move.

( ) ⓓ Little Thunder's finger felt cool.

(1) ⓔ Little Thunder came to the forest clearing.

( ) ⓕ Little Thunder waited on the ground.

( ) ⓖ Little Thunder dropped to the ground.

(2) Which of the following is Little Thunder most likely to do next? Put a check (✓) next to the best answer.

( ) ⓐ Little Thunder goes swimming.

( ) ⓑ Little Thunder tries to catch the animal in the grass.

( ) ⓒ Little Thunder runs away.

2 Read the passage and then answer the questions below.

Little Thunder was ready to let his sharpest arrow fly when he saw a newborn baby fawn. He put the arrow in its pouch and moved slowly toward her. The frightened animal was trying to stand on her thin legs when they buckled and she fell down. He didn't mean to scare the struggling animal when he laughed.

She tried again, but her legs wouldn't support her body. The boy walked over to make sure she wasn't hurt. He reached out to touch her soft new fur. As he was stroking her, he could feel her calm down. Then he felt her rough little tongue lapping at his cheek.

(1) What is a good title for this passage? Put a check (✓) next to the best title.

10 points

( ) ⓐ Little Thunder's Surprise

( ) ⓑ Little Thunder Makes a Big Catch

( ) ⓒ Little Thunder is a Big Hunter

(2) Choose the best answer to each question below. Write the letter in the space provided.

10 points per question

① What was the little fawn trying to do?

ⓐ The little fawn was trying to stand up.

ⓑ The little fawn was trying to sleep.

ⓒ The little fawn was trying to eat.   (   )

② What could the boy feel as he was stroking the animal?

ⓐ He could feel her tired legs.

ⓑ He could feel her getting scared.

ⓒ He could feel her calming down.   (   )

③ Which of these sentences would be the best next line?

ⓐ Little Thunder continued hunting.

ⓑ Little Thunder had made a friend.

ⓒ Little Thunder did not understand.   (   )   Way to go!

Revising Predictions
Alonzo and Summer Camp

26

Level
★★★

Score

/100

Date   /   /

Name

1 Read the passage and then answer the questions below.

10 points per question

It was the last day of school and Alonzo was on the bus. He knew his mother would soon ask him if he wanted to go to summer camp. As the city flew by in a blur, he started to think about last year's summer camp.

He remembered arriving and how scared he was. He did not know anyone, and he had not been away from home before. He remembered wondering if everyone else felt the same way. All the other children seemed to know someone.

As he unpacked his clothes, his roommate came in. His name was Jack and it was his second year. Jack threw all his clothes in one drawer and ran out to meet his friends without saying hello to Alonzo.

(1) When and where did this story begin?

This story began on the _____ with Alonzo

on _____.

(2) Why was Alonzo scared when he arrived at camp last year?

Alonzo was scared because he did not _____ and had

not _____ before.

(3) Do you think Jack is going to be friendly with Alonzo?

_____, because Jack ran out to meet _____ without

_____ to Alonzo.

(4) Which of these sentences would be the best next line? Put a check (✓) next to the best line.

(   ) ⓐ Alonzo already wanted to go home.

(   ) ⓑ Alonzo wanted a hamburger.

(   ) ⓒ Alonzo smiled.

Read the passage and then answer the questions below.

12 points per question

Alonzo remembered how alone he felt that first day at camp. Instead of going outside, he pulled out a book and sat on his bed. At least he had a book that he liked to keep himself company! He began reading, but he kept hearing all the boys playing outside.

Just as Alonzo was about to put down his book and go outside, Jack came back in.

"Hi there!" Jack said, out of breath.

"Hello," answered Alonzo timidly. He wasn't feeling very sure of himself.

"I'm sorry I didn't say hello before," Jack said. "I just saw a friend and wanted to say hello right away!" he continued.

"That's okay," Alonzo said, feeling better.

"Oh! My name is Jack!" Jack blurted out.

"My name is Alonzo," said Alonzo.

"Sooo.. Did you bring a baseball? I like to play catch but forgot to bring a baseball!" said Jack, who seemed to have a lot of energy.

"Actually, I did!" said Alonzo, and they ran outside to play catch in the summer sun.

(1) What did Alonzo do at first?

He _____ and _____.

(2) Why did Alonzo answer Jack timidly?

He wasn't _____.

(3) Why did Jack leave before saying hello?

Jack left before saying hello because he just _____

and _____ right away.

(4) What did Jack ask Alonzo?

Jack asked Alonzo if he brought a _____ because he

_____ one.

(5) Do you think that Alonzo will go to summer camp again this year?

_____.

Do you like summer camp?

Reading Comprehension
What a Day at the Zoo! 1

Level ★★★

Date / /

Name

Score /100

1 Read the passage and answer the questions below using words from the passage.

12 points per question

> Josh couldn't sit still in the car. He was going to the zoo with his family!
>
> Josh thought the best animal was the tiger. It was scary, but it was also very pretty with all its stripes. Josh daydreamed about a tiger having breakfast with him in the morning. They were eating pancakes and the tiger was very hungry.
>
> "Now, Josh, make sure you don't get lost today," said his mother, interrupting his dream.
>
> "Okay, Mom," said Josh, but he really was thinking about putting strawberries on the tiger's pancakes.
>
> "Mom, can we see the tiger first?" asked Josh hopefully.
>
> "Don't you want to see the birds?" asked his mother. She liked the birds best of all.
>
> "No, birds are boring!" responded Josh.

(1) What animal did Josh think was the best?

Josh thought that the _____ was the best animal.

(2) Why was the tiger Josh's favorite animal?

The tiger was Josh's favorite animal because it was _____ but also

very _____.

(3) What did Josh have for breakfast in his daydream?

Josh had _____ for breakfast in his daydream.

(4) Was Josh listening to his mom?

_____, Josh was really thinking about _____

on the tiger's pancakes.

(5) How did Josh ask about seeing the tiger first?

Josh asked _____ if they could _____.

2 Read the passage. Then number the pictures to match the order they occur in the passage.

40 points for completion

It seemed that everything took forever. He wanted to be inside the zoo already. He didn't want to be parking the car. He didn't want to be waiting in line. He didn't want to be waiting for a tour.

"Okay, let's just go," his father said finally, and they were off!

First, they visited the birds like his mother wanted. Some were very colorful, and all of them were loud. But none of the birds were scary.

Then they saw the snakes. The snakes were scary, but not very pretty, thought Josh. They saw the frogs next. The frogs were slimy, but not scary or pretty.

He liked the otters. They looked like little water cats!

They took a break for a little lunch. Sitting on the bench, Josh watched all sorts of people walk by as he ate his snack. People are animals too! They are not as nice looking as tigers, though, he thought.

After lunch, they visited the monkeys. The monkeys made funny noises and Josh liked the way they swung on the trees. He watched them for a while, and when he turned around, his parents were gone.

"Uh-oh," Josh said out loud. Where did they go?

(1) (　　) (2) (　　) (3) (　　) (4) (　　)

(5) (　　) (6) (　　) (7) (　　) (8) (　　)

What do you think is the best animal?

Reading Comprehension
What a Day at the Zoo! 2

Level ★★★

Score

28

Date / /

Name

/100

1 Read the passage and answer the questions below using words from the passage.

12 points per question

Where did they go? Josh was lost. He looked back by the snakes, but his parents weren't there. They weren't by the otters or the monkeys. They weren't by the birds either.

Josh did not know what to do. He remembered that he had not yet seen the tiger, so he thought maybe he should look by the tiger. That way he would see the tiger and maybe find his parents too.

But his parents were not by the tiger. Josh started getting sad. The tiger seemed to understand. Josh looked at him with tears in his eyes.

"Why are you so sad?" asked the tiger.

"What? Tigers can't talk," said Josh.

"You learn something new every day," responded the tiger. "So why are you so sad?"

"I lost my parents!" said Josh.

(1) What happened to Josh?

Josh was _____.

(2) Where did Josh look first for his parents?

He looked back by the _____, the _____, the _____

and the _____.

(3) Why did Josh decide to go to the tiger?

Josh decided to go to the tiger so that he would _____

and maybe find _____, too.

(4) What did Josh say to the tiger at first?

Josh said that _____.

(5) Which is the best title for this section of the story? Put a (✓) next to the best title.

( ) ⓐ Tigers are Better than Birds

( ) ⓑ Where are Josh's Parents?

( ) ⓒ Tigers Can't Talk

Read the passage. Then answer the questions below.

"Well, that's too bad. I lost my parents, too," said the tiger.

"You did?" asked Josh hopefully.

"Yup, and I've been fine without them," answered the tiger proudly.

That made Josh cry. He was not going to be fine without his parents.

The tiger did not understand. He just kept looking at Josh as if he was a strange animal.

"You silly tiger, did you make that child cry?" said someone.

"Oh, be quiet, you noisy parrot," said the tiger back.

"I lost my parents!" said Josh to the parrot.

"Oh, that is very sad! And you did not offer to help him, you mean tiger?" said the parrot. The tiger didn't answer, and just sat in the shade.

"I will help you!" said the parrot. "Tell me what your parents are wearing!" Josh told the parrot, and the bird flew all over the zoo.

The parrot came back and Josh followed him to his parents. They were very happy to find him, but Josh turned around and thanked the parrot who found his parents with a little bow. Then he hugged his parents hard.

"You know," said Josh, "I think I like birds after all."

(1) How did the tiger answer Josh?

The tiger answered Josh _____.

(2) How did the tiger show that he did not understand why Josh was upset?

The tiger just kept _____ as if he was a _____.

(3) Who asked the tiger if he made Josh cry?

The _____ if he made Josh cry.

(4) What did Josh do before he hugged his parents?

Josh turned around and _____ with a _____.

(5) Why did Josh change his mind about birds?

Josh changed his mind because

_____.

Way to go!
You are a star reader!

Reading Comprehension
The King Has No Clothes 1

Level ★★★

Score /100

Date / /

Name

1 Read the passage. Then answer the questions using full sentences and correct verb tenses.

12 points per question

> Once there was an unusual king. He wasn't like other rulers. He cared only for clothes. He loved clothes. He was never happier than when he was getting new clothes! They were all that he thought about and cared about. He wore a new suit at each meal.
>
> If people wanted to find him, they just checked his dressing room. While he was busy with his wardrobe, he let other people run his land. One day, a pair of tricksters came to the palace. They told the people of the court that they were fine tailors and wanted to make the king some new clothes. No one expected them to be jokers.

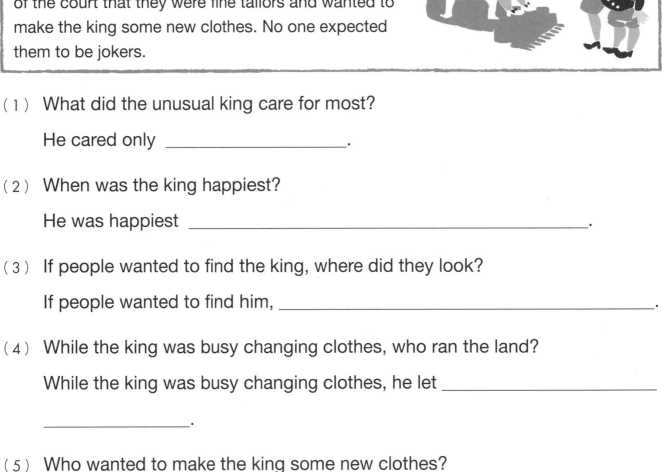

(1) What did the unusual king care for most?

He cared only _____.

(2) When was the king happiest?

He was happiest _____.

(3) If people wanted to find the king, where did they look?

If people wanted to find him, _____.

(4) While the king was busy changing clothes, who ran the land?

While the king was busy changing clothes, he let _____

_____.

(5) Who wanted to make the king some new clothes?

A pair _____ wanted to _____.

2 Read the passage. Then answer the questions below.

The tricksters said they wove their cloth from only the finest thread. The material was as unusual as it was costly, the tailors explained. Their cloth came from far-away kingdoms. It had the brightest colors and boldest shapes in all the land. It was soft. The most unusual thing about the cloth was that fools who were not fit for their jobs would not be able to see it. The king hired the tricky tailors at once.

The king wanted to know if the people who ran his land were fit for their jobs. With these clothes, he could find all the fools in his court. For that, he would pay any price.

The tailor shop was set up right away. The tailors were given the biggest and best looms* to create clothes from their special cloth.

*loom – machine for weaving

(1) What was the most unusual thing about the tricksters' cloth?

Fools who were not _____ would

not _____.

(2) When did the king hire the tailors?

The king hired them _____.

(3) Why did the king want this special cloth?

The king wanted this special cloth because he wanted to know if the

_____ were _____.

(4) What things were given to the two tricksters?

_____ were given to the two

tricksters.

Do you like getting new clothes?

30

Date   /   /

Name

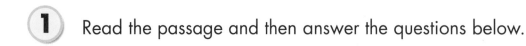

1 Read the passage and then answer the questions below.

What the two men were really doing was pretending! They just moved their hands through the empty air. Day and night they ate and slept in the palace and did nothing. For months, the king paid for their costly food and wine.

At last, the door of the shop was opened. Everyone expected to see yards and yards of cloth, but the shelves were empty.

"How do you like it?" asked the tricky tailors.

There was nothing to see, but no one said anything. The knights did not want to be seen as fools or as unfit for their jobs.

"It's the most magical cloth," they lied.

When the king walked in, his eyes opened wide. Where was the new cloth? Afraid he would be called a fool, he didn't say a word.

"Incredible!" he cried. "Make me a new suit for the royal parade next week!"

(1) Fill in the charts using words from the story.   8 points per question

How the Tricksters Pretended:
They moved ①_____ .
They asked how people liked the invisible ②_____ on the ③_____ shelves.

Who Else Pretended to See the Clothes:
The ④_____ said the cloth was magical.
The ⑤_____ asked for a new suit.

(2) Answer the question below in your own words.   20 points

Do you think anyone will be able to see the fabric? Why?

_____, I don't think anyone will be able to see the fabric because _____
_____ .

2 Read the passage and then answer the questions below.

The tailors pretended to measure, cut, and stitch clothes for the king. The king got ready to wear the new clothes. The tailors moved their hands as if they were putting the invisible suit on the king. The king looked in the mirror, but he saw only himself and his underwear.

"It looks good, don't you think?"

"Of course!" the tailors smiled.

"Then I am ready for the parade," sighed the king.

In the crowd, there was a little boy who was more honest than anyone else dared to be. He called out, "The king is not wearing any clothes!"

The people started to laugh. The king's face turned red. His own foolishness had been shown by a little boy.

From then on, the king was known as "The King with No Clothes." He hoped his people would forget that day, but they never did!

(1) How did the tailors pretend to make the suit fit the king?

The tailors pretended to _____

for the king.

(2) What did the king see in the mirror?

The king saw only _____ in the

mirror.

(3) Why did the little boy say what he did?

The little boy was _____ than _____.

(4) Why did the king's face turn red?

The king's face turned red because

_____

_____.

You're doing great!

Reading Comprehension
The Chinese Artists 1

31

Level ★★★

Score

Date / /

Name

/100

1 Read the passage and then answer the questions below.

8 points per question

> Long ago in China there lived a young boy named Yan. Yan had no family and no home. In return for food, he worked at Dadan's art school. Dadan was not a very good painter, although he tried to hide it. He was also rather nasty because he often lied.
>
> Every day, Yan worked hard for Dadan. Every night, Yan spent hours looking at the many paintings by different artists that hung on the walls. His favorite painting was by Rong-Wu, China's greatest painter, and was of a beautiful garden. The garden was filled with unusual flowers and trees. Around the outside ran a wall with a little door.
>
> The painting was valuable to Dadan for many reasons. It was worth a lot of money, but it also came with a mysterious story.

(1) Where did Yan work?

Yan worked _____.

(2) Who was not a very good painter?

_____ a very good painter.

(3) Why was Dadan nasty?

Dadan was nasty because he _____.

(4) When did Yan look at Dadan's paintings?

_____, Yan looked at Dadan's pantings.

(5) What did Rong-Wu paint?

Rong-Wu painted a beautiful _____.

2 Read the passage and answer the questions below.

Three hundred years ago, the Emperor asked Rong-Wu to create a picture to hang in the palace. When old Rong-Wu finished, he said, "What a wonderful resting place that would be." Then he walked into the painting. He closed the little garden door and was never seen again.

After seeing that painting, Yan decided to paint, too. He asked Dadan to teach him, but Dadan would not. "Then I will teach myself!" thought Yan. While he worked, he listened to Dadan's lessons. He learned the names of the great painters. He watched the students work.

At night, Yan would sit in front of Rong-Wu's famous garden and try to paint. Unsure of himself, he would paint only a few strokes. "I wish I had a teacher!" he cried.

Yan stared in disbelief as the painted garden door opened and the great Rong-Wu appeared. Smiling gently, Rong-Wu said, "Do not be afraid to come with me."

(1) Fill in the chart using text from the passage.

How Yan Learned to Paint
Yan taught himself. Yan listened to ①_____.
Yan watched ②_____.

(2) Compare and contrast Dadan and Rong-Wu.
Write a "**D**" next to the statements that describe Dadan, and an "**R**" next to the statements that describe Rong-Wu. (Hint: You can look on p. 62, too.)

(   ) ① was not a very good painter.   (   ) ③ lied and was nasty.

(   ) ② was China's greatest painter.   (   ) ④ smiled gently.

(3) Based on your answers to (2), do you think Yan will follow Rong-Wu? Why?
Answer in your own words.

I think _____

_____ .

Do not be afraid to write your best guess!

32

Date / /

Name

1 Read the passage and then answer the questions below.

As frightened as he was, Yan leapt to his feet and followed Rong-Wu into the painted garden. It was dawn before he came back out.

Every night after that, Yan returned to the painting and knocked on the door. The door would always open, and Yan would always enter. Soon, Yan's eyes grew bright with excitement and hope, instead of seeming dull and hopeless. He held himself proudly and walked confidently. He no longer shook with fear when Dadan shouted at him for being slow. One day the angry Dadan decided to follow Yan.

When Dadan saw Yan walk arm-in-arm with Rong-Wu into the painting, he became even angrier! He ran wildly about the room. He screamed. He howled. Then he grabbed his paints and brushes. Upon the priceless Rong-Wu painting itself, Dadan painted one brick after another until a solid wall blocked the garden's only exit.

(1) Fill in the chart below.

5 points per question

Old Yan	New Yan
eyes seeming ①_____ and hopeless	eyes bright with excitement and ②_____
shook with ③_____	proud and ④_____

(2) Write the word in the passage that matches the following definition.

10 points

valuable, worth a lot of money, cannot be given a price   (   )

(3) When did Dadan get angry?

10 points

Dadan got angry when Yan no longer _____ when being yelled at.

(4) What made Dadan even angrier?

10 points

Dadan became angrier when he saw Yan _____ with Rong-Wu.

2 Read the passage and then answer the questions below.

10 points per question

Ten years passed, and nobody saw Yan. Dadan grew nastier and nastier, until one day which nobody would ever forget. Dadan had been standing in front of the Rong-Wu painting, talking to his students. One by one, bricks of the wall in the painting began to wiggle and fall into the room with a loud clunk. Soon a large hole appeared. Out stepped an older and taller Yan, with hundreds of paintings rolled under his arm.

"We are ready to show our paintings, Rong-Wu," he called, but Rong-Wu only shook his head gently.

"I am too old and tired to paint. You must do it for me," said Rong-Wu. With that, he closed the painted door behind him forever.

Yan cried, but with the lessons of Rong-Wu in his heart and in his brush, he knew he was ready for the next step.

In fear, Dadan ran away from the art school, never to be seen again.

(1) As ten years passed, what happened to Dadan?

As ten years passed, Dadan grew _____.

(2) What happened on the unforgettable day?

On the unforgettable day, the bricks that Dadan had painted on Rong-Wu's

painting began _____ into the room.

(3) What did Yan carry under his arm?

Yan carried _____ rolled under his arm.

(4) Where did Yan carry Rong-Wu's lessons?

Yan carried his lessons in _____ and in _____.

(5) Was Dadan ever seen again?

_____.

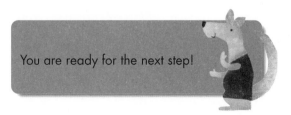

You are ready for the next step!

Reading Comprehension
Wonder Kid Meets the Evil Lunch Snatcher 1

33

Level ★★★

Score

/100

Date / /

Name

1 Read the passage below from *Wonder Kid Meets the Evil Lunch Snatcher* by Lois Duncan. Then answer the questions below.

12 points per question

Brian raced through the opening in the hedge and burst out onto the playground.

What he saw there stopped him dead in his tracks.

Sarah was surrounded by a group of five tough-looking boys.

The largest of them had thick, black hair that stood up on his head in spikes. In his hand he was holding a brown paper sack.

"What are you doing with my sister's lunch?" cried Brian. He wanted his voice to sound threatening, but it squeaked in a funny way.

"This isn't your sister's lunch anymore," said the boy. He opened the sack and began to rummage inside it. "Hey, look what a lot of stuff she has in here! Five chocolate chip cookies! That's one for each of us."

He took a bite of one cookie and tossed the others to his friends.

They all popped them into their mouths and started chewing.

---

(1) Where did Brian enter the playground?

Brian entered the playground through _____.

(2) Who was Sarah surrounded by?

Sarah was surrounded by _____.

(3) How did Brian want his voice to sound?

Brian wanted his voice _____.

(4) What did the largest boy do to Sarah's lunch sack?

He opened the sack and _____.

(5) When did the largest boy start chewing the cookie?

He started to chew the cookie when he tossed _____

to _____.

2 Read the passage and then answer the questions below.

10 points per question

"You robbers!" Sarah exploded. "Those cookies are mine!"

"I always like to eat dessert first," said the boy. "Now let's see what you've brought for my main course." He reached into the sack again and pulled more things out. "An apple, chips, and a sandwich. I wonder what kind it is." He unwrapped the sandwich and held it up to his nose. "Yuck! It smells like tuna. I can't stand tuna."

He dropped the sandwich onto the ground and put his foot on it.

The tuna filling squished out on both sides of his shoe.

Brian stared at the boy in disbelief.

"You can't do that!" he exclaimed. "You're wrecking her lunch!"

"That's a punishment for breaking the rules," said the boy.

"What rules?" cried Sarah. "I didn't do anything wrong!"

"You came through the Sixth-Grade Gate," the boy told her. "Only big kids are allowed to come in this entrance."

(1) How did the boy treat the tuna sandwich?

He _____ it onto _____ and _____ on it.

(2) How did Brian look at the boy?

Brian stared _____.

(3) Why did the boy say he was wrecking Sarah's lunch?

He said it was a _____ for _____.

(4) What rule did Sarah break?

She came through the _____.

Hey, I like tuna!

67

34

Reading Comprehension
Wonder Kid Meets the Evil Lunch Snatcher 2

Level ★★★

Date   /   /

Name

Score   /100

1 Read the passage and then fill in the charts using words from the passage.

30 points per question

… "Come on, Sarah," said Brian, grabbing his sister's hand.

He backed through the hole in the hedge, dragging Sarah with him.

I ought to be standing up to that creep, he thought miserably. The kids at my old school were right when they called me a wimp!

"So the lunch-snatcher gang got two new victims!" a voice said.

Brian spun around to find a boy watching him from the sidewalk. The boy had curly red hair and was wearing glasses.

"The other day I forgot and went in through that gate," he said. "Matt and his gang pulled my lunch apart and stamped on it." …

Brian was so shocked he could hardly speak. "Can't *anybody* do *anything*? That guy's a *criminal*!"

The boy shook his head. "Matt runs the school. It would take a superhero to bring him to justice."

"It would take a …what?" Brian couldn't believe what he'd heard.

(1)

What the kids at Brian's old school called him	a ①_____
What Brian thought of Matt	a ②_____ , a ③_____
What the curly-haired boy called the five tough-looking boys	the ④_____
What the curly-haired boy called Brian and Sarah	two ⑤_____

(2)

What Brian Did
①_____ through the hole in ②_____
dragged ③_____ with him
④_____ around
met a boy with ⑤_____ hair who wore ⑥_____

Read the passage and answer the questions below.

"A superhero," the boy repeated. "You know — like Batman. Or Plastic Man or Wonder Woman or —"

He broke off suddenly as though he were afraid Brian would make fun of him.

"Or Captain Marvel," said Brian. "Or Spiderman or Superman."

The red-haired boy stared at him in astonishment.

"Do you read comic books, too?"

"I have a whole collection," said Brian. "My dad calls them junk, but I feel good when I read them."

"I know. They make you feel powerful," the boy said, nodding. "My name's Robbie Chandler. I'm in fourth grade."

"I'm Brian Johnson," said Brian. "I'm in fourth grade, too."

From behind the hedge, there came the sound of the bell again.

"That's the second bell!" shrieked Sarah. "Now we're *really* late!"

"We're late, agreed Robbie. "But we're all of us late together."

All of a sudden Brian found himself feeling much better.

(1) How did the red-haired boy look at Brian after he mentioned Superman?

The red-haired boy _____.

(2) How do comics make Robbie feel?

Comics make Robbie _____.

(3) Why doesn't Brian worry about the second bell as much as Sarah?

Brian doesn't worry as much because Robbie said they are all

_____.

(4) How did Brian feel after Robbie said they would be late?

All of a sudden, Brian felt

_____.

Talk to your parents about who you think will be the Wonder Boy, or read the rest of the book!

Level ★★

Score /100

Date / /

Name

1 Use the words given to complete the sentences below.

5 points per question

(1) [big / bigger / biggest]

Farmer Brown has a _____ dog. His goat is _____, though.

His bull is the _____ animal he owns.

(2) [happy / happier / happiest]

Reading books makes me _____. I'm even _____ when I get

to read on the beach. I'm _____ when I get ice cream, though.

(3) [help / helpful / helpless]

Mom asked me to _____ make dinner. Although I like to be

_____, I don't know how to make dinner by myself. Then I'm

_____.

(4) [care / careful / careless]

When you are swimming, you have to be _____. You have to take

_____ when you are near the diving board. Don't be _____!

(5) [hungry / hungrily]

Susan did not have lunch and was _____! When she got home,

she _____ ate a whole fruit salad.

2 Read the sentences. If both underlined words mean the **same**, circle the **"S."**
If the words are **opposites**, circle the **"O."**

5 points per question

(1) Right when I <u>arrive</u>, you <u>leave</u>. Where do you go? **S**   **O**

(2) Bill <u>likes</u> chocolate ice cream. His brother <u>enjoys</u> vanilla. **S**   **O**

(3) Sue thinks the movie is <u>boring</u>. Dana finds it <u>interesting</u>. **S**   **O**

(4) What a <u>pretty</u> comb! Where did you get such a <u>beautiful</u> thing? **S**   **O**

(5) Many things that were once <u>built</u> have been <u>destroyed</u>. **S**   **O**

3 Read the following sentences. Then pick the word from each sentence that completes the definition below.

5 points per question

(1) My mother is small, but she prefers to be called petite.

_____ means small in size

(2) Fela offered some of his curry to Zack, but he refused.

_____ means to have said no to something

(3) Josh liked the unusual comic books because they were not boring.

_____ means different or unique

(4) Farmer Hernandez makes sure to harvest his watermelons in the summer because that is when they are the sweetest.

_____ means to gather a vegetable or fruit from the field

4 Read the passage. Then answer the questions using text from the passage.

15 points per question

Where were the fawn's parents? Little Thunder searched far and wide. He followed some tracks down to the lake's edge, and climbed a tree to look over the grasslands, but he could not find the fawn's parents.

The boy ran back to the little fawn. He carried the animal to a nearby cave. Every day he returned, bringing her food and water until she was able to walk on her own. They played games together and he taught her to come to him when he whistled. Then one day the tribe had to move on to find a better place to live during the winter weather. Little Thunder said goodbye to his new friend, who had grown stronger over the weeks.

(1) Where did Little Thunder search for the fawn's parents?

Little Thunder went down _____ and climbed

_____ to _____ for the

fawn's parents.

(2) What did Little Thunder teach the little fawn?

Little Thunder taught her _____

_____.

Good job!

1 Read the passage and then answer the questions below.

12 points per question

> Many months later, when his tribe had returned, Little Thunder found the same clearing that he had come upon a long time ago. He was chasing a full-grown deer when it turned around and stared at him. Little Thunder was about to take aim when instead, he whistled softly. The deer approached the boy and began licking his cheek! They were reunited! Little Thunder was glad that he did not hurt the deer he had known for so long.

(1) What did Little Thunder do instead of taking aim?

Instead of taking aim, Little Thunder _____.

(2) Which sentence would be a good last sentence for this story? Put a check (✓) next to the best sentence.

( ) ⓐ The deer hunted with Little Thunder.

( ) ⓑ The deer ran away from Little Thunder.

( ) ⓒ The deer went back into the woods where she still lives in peace.

2 Read the passage and then complete the chart below.

4 points per question

> Julie's mom asked her to go shopping for dinner. She gave her a list that had the amount of each item she should get and how much they would each cost. She told her to get three apples that would cost about one dollar, and twelve carrots for about two dollars. Then she was supposed to get three fish for twelve dollars. She also had to get one bottle of olive oil for four dollars.

Food	Number	Price
Apples	(1)	$1
(2)	12	(3) $ ___
(4)	(5)	$12
Olive (6) _____	1	(7) $ ___

3 Read the story and answer the questions below.

> Maria was having a bad day. She forgot her lunch in the morning, and that was only the start of things. When she went back to get her lunch, the bus left without her. Then her mother was angry. Since she had to drive Maria to school, her mother was going to be late for work, too.
>
> After all that, Maria left her lunch in the car. She did not know where her mind was! In English class, she stumbled over the words and did not read her passage very well. She was sure she would get a bad grade.
>
> She had to borrow some lunch from her friends who made fun of her. They were not helping. They played dodgeball in gym class, and she fell and skinned her knee. The day could not get any worse.
>
> She was ready to cry when she got home. Then she saw that her mother had made her favorite food, fish tacos, and was ready to listen. Everything would be okay.

(1) Number the sentences below to match the order they happen in the story.

( ) ⓐ Maria fell during gym class.

( ) ⓑ Maria's mother made fish tacos.

( ) ⓒ Maria missed the bus.

( ) ⓓ Maria had to borrow lunch.

( ) ⓔ Maria's mother drove her to school.

( ) ⓕ Maria did not read her passage well.

(2) Why was Maria's mother angry?

Maria's mother was angry because she had to _____

and she was going to be _____, too.

(3) Why did Maria think everything was going to be okay?

Maria thought everything was going to be okay because _____

_____ food and was _____.

You did it! Good job!

1 Prefixes pp 2,3

1 (1) up / hill / uphill (2) hill
(3) doors (4) outdoors

2 (1) ⓒ (2) ⓕ
(3) ⓐ (4) ⓔ
(5) ⓓ (6) ⓑ

3 undo, redo, untie, retie, reuse, unusual

4 (1) retie (2) redo
(3) unlock (4) repay
(5) untie (6) reuse
(7) unhappy (8) unpack

2 Suffixes pp 4,5

1 (1) fast (2) faster
(3) fastest (4) high
(5) higher (6) highest
(7) young (8) younger
(9) youngest

2 B

3 (1) ① sunny ② sunnier
(2) ① bigger ② biggest
(3) ① happier ② happiest

4 (1) biggest pumpkin
(2) strawberry is sweetest
(3) will be fun

3 Suffixes pp 6,7

1 (1) use / useful / useless
(2) help / helpful / helpless

2 (1) color / colorful
(2) fear / fearless
(3) useful / use / useless
(4) helpful / help / helpless
(5) careless / care / careful

3 (1) neat
(2) noisily
(3) busy
(4) hungrily

4 (1) happy / happily
(2) heavy / heavily
(3) light / lightly
(4) quick / quickly
(5) thirsty / thirstily

4 Compare pp 8,9

1 (1) ⓒ (2) ⓕ
(3) ⓔ (4) ⓑ
(5) ⓐ (6) ⓓ

2 (1) answer (2) small
(3) like (4) last
(5) shout

3 (1), (2), (3), (4)

4 (1) wardrobe (2) knights
(3) tailors (4) tricksters

5 Contrast pp 10,11

1 (1) ⓒ (2) ⓑ
(3) ⓓ (4) ⓐ
(5) ⓔ (6) ⓕ

2 (1) continue (2) took
(3) tiny (4) destroyed
(5) won (6) asked
(7) frown (8) found

3 (1) same (2) evening
(3) destroyed (4) laughed
(5) exit

4 (1) found (2) worse
(3) sink (4) arrive
(5) disappear

6 Compare & Contrast
pp 12,13

1 (1) O   (2) O
   (3) S   (4) S
   (5) O   (6) S

2 (1) large   (2) sour
   (3) cried   (4) fast
   (5) smart   (6) first

3 (1) wakes   (2) falls asleep
   (3) after   (4) wastes time

4 (1) larger   (2) short
   (3) fly   (4) white

7 Defining Words by Context
pp 14,15

1 (1) height   (2) stumble
   (3) solve

2 (1) vanilla   (2) appetite
   (3) spaghetti   (4) fingernails
   (5) weary

3 (1) happiness   (2) spun
   (3) small   (4) blossom

4 (1) ⓔ   (2) ⓓ
   (3) ⓐ   (4) ⓕ
   (5) ⓒ   (6) ⓑ

8 Defining Words by Context
pp 16,17

1 (1) karate   (2) apologize
   (3) collect   (4) sturdy

2 (1) subway   (2) arrive
   (3) barefoot   (4) helmet
   (5) boring   (6) nonsense

3 (1) relax   (2) curious
   (3) imagine   (4) routine

4 (1) wrecked   (2) overboard
   (3) choppy   (4) thicket

9 Defining Words by Context
pp 18,19

1 (1) unbearable   (2) passengers
   (3) aisle   (4) journey
   (5) comfortable

2 (1) snowball   (2) iceberg
   (3) shivering   (4) fireplace

3 (1) office   (2) chef
   (3) scrambled   (4) celebrate
   (5) soccer   (6) chopsticks
   (7) crouched

10 Defining Words by Context
pp 20,21

1 (1) excited
   (2) astronaut
   (3) explore

2 (1) clever   (2) identical
   (3) sidewalk   (4) adventure

3 (1) astronauts   (2) escaped
   (3) adventure   (4) comfortable
   (5) sidewalk   (6) passengers

4 (1) explored   (2) identical
   (3) clever   (4) station
   (5) chased   (6) excited

11 Vocabulary Review
pp 22,23

1 redo, quickly, unhappy, upstairs, carefully, careless, undo, freshest, hopefully, hopeless (possible answer)

2 (1) CURIOUS   (2) FOOTBALL
   (3) LOCATE   (4) IMAGINE
   (5) ORIGINAL   (6) COMPASS
   (7) UPHILL   (8) COMFORTABLE

12 Who/What/When/Where pp 24, 25

1 (1) Samson
(2) comics / video games
(3) rises at dawn
(4) kitchen / morning light
(5) every day / getting ready for school / never cleans his room

2 (1) Her homework is always <u>organized</u>.
(2) ① in the morning
② Angela
③ help him study
④ play video games

13 Who/What/When/Where pp 26, 27

1 (1) a soft blanket and pillow
(2) they work hard
(3) seaweed / top of the sea
(4) sharks / swimming
(5) clown fish

2 (1) frogs
(2) two openings
(3) Foxes
(4) fall asleep
(5) leaf / branch

14 Who/What/When/Where pp 28, 29

1 (1) run fast
(2) brown spots
(3) 1940
(4) grass
(5) kings and rulers

2 (1) young man / next emperor
(2) the other boys' plants grew taller and taller
(3) brave enough / only the truth

15 Who/What/When/Where/Why pp 30, 31

1 (1) president / his family
(2) White House / built
(3) George Washington
(4) was not finished
(5) John Adams

2 (1) burned down
(2) Office space
(3) West Wing
(4) Harry Truman
(5) 140

16 Who/What/When/Where/Why/How pp 32, 33

1 (1) <u>Karen</u>
(2) ① purple sweater
② never wanted to wear the sweater
③ wear purple
④ quickly

2 (1) cold (2) mother
(3) hastily (4) proud
(5) slowly

17 Vocabulary Review pp 34, 35

1 (1) expanded (2) rare
(3) cheetah (4) crouched
(5) results (6) beautiful

2 (1) blanket (2) sweater
(3) president (4) office
(5) dangerous (6) champions

3 (1) PLAYFUL (2) UNDERGROUND
(3) HAPPIEST (4) ESCAPED
(5) SURPRISED (6) CHORES
(7) IMPORTANT (8) ORGANIZED

18 Chart the Passage
pp 36, 37

1 (1) How to Get Ready to Cook Dinner

(2) Things They Got at the Grocery Store

2 (1) onions (2) carrots (3) pepper (4) fish

(5) Salad (6) bell (7) spinach

(8) strawberries (9) sugar

19 Chart the Passage
pp 38, 39

1 (1) How People Planned Their Days Long Ago

(2) How a Sundial Works

2 (1) plowing (2) oats (3) weeds (4) hay

(5) grains (6) shade (7) picking (8) planting

(9) firewood (10) weaving

20 Chart the Passage
pp 40, 41

1 (1) Why a Ski Vacation Was Going to Be Fun

(2) Ski Equipment

2 (1) ① very long

② cried

(2) ① stop faster

② turns better

21 Chart the Passage
pp 42, 43

1 (1) Nile

(2) Brazil

(3) 4,082 miles

(4) U.S.A.

2 (1) NAME

(2) Poseidon

(3) messenger (of the gods)

(4) Cupid

3 (1) ① fifth ② over sixty-three ③ red spot

(2) ① sixth ② sixty-one ③ rings

(3) ⓐ

22 Chart the Passage
pp 44, 45

1 (1) ① seeds

② Sparrow

③ worms

④ blue

⑤ Woodpecker

⑥ insects

(2) ⓒ

2 (1) (1) big

(2) day

(3) biggest

(4) owls

(5) night

(6) poles

(7) cliffs

(8) barns

(2) ⓐ

23 Chart the Passage
pp 46, 47

1 (1) ① soup

② pizza

③ sandwich

(2) ⓒ

2 (1) ① video games

② comic books

③ Kim's bike

④ reading

⑤ spaghetti

24 Sequencing
pp 48, 49

1 (1) 7 (2) 5 (3) 1 (4) 2 (5) 9 (6) 3 (7) 6 (8) 4

(9) 8

2 (1) ⓐ 8 ⓑ 5 ⓒ 7 ⓓ 4 ⓔ 2 ⓕ 3 ⓖ 6 ⓗ 1

(2) ⓒ

25 Making Predictions
pp 50,51

1 (1) ⓐ 6 ⓑ 5 ⓒ 2 ⓓ 7 ⓔ 1 ⓕ 4 ⓖ 3

(2) ⓑ

2 (1) ⓐ

(2) ① ⓐ

② ⓒ

③ ⓑ

26 Revising Predictions
pp 52,53

1 (1) last day of school / the bus

(2) know anyone / been away from home

(3) No / his friends / saying hello

(4) ⓐ

2 (1) pulled out a book / sat on his bed

(2) feeling very sure of himself

(3) saw a friend / wanted to say hello

(4) baseball / forgot to bring

(5) Yes

27 Reading Comprehension
pp 54,55

1 (1) tiger

(2) scary / pretty

(3) pancakes

(4) No / putting strawberries

(5) hopefully / see the tiger first

2 (1) 8 (2) 1 (3) 5 (4) 3 (5) 4 (6) 6 (7) 2 (8) 7

28 Reading Comprehension
pp 56,57

1 (1) lost

(2) snakes / otters / monkeys / birds

(3) see the tiger / his parents

(4) tigers can't talk

(5) ⓑ

2 (1) proudly

(2) looking at Josh / strange animal

(3) parrot asked the tiger

(4) thanked the parrot / little bow

(5) the parrot found his parents

29 Reading Comprehension
pp 58,59

1 (1) for clothes

(2) when he was getting new clothes

(3) they just checked his dressing room

(4) other people run his land

(5) of tricksters / make the king some new clothes

2 (1) fit for their jobs / be able to see it

(2) at once

(3) people who ran his land / fit for their jobs

(4) The biggest and best looms

30 Reading Comprehension
pp 60,61

1 (1) ① their hands through the empty air

② cloth

③ empty

④ knights

⑤ king

(2) No / the tricksters didn't really make anything (possible answer)

2 (1) measure, cut, and stitch clothes

(2) himself and his underwear

(3) more honest / anyone else dared to be

(4) his own foolishness had been shown by a little boy

31 Reading Comprehension   pp 62,63

1 (1) at Dadan's art school
  (2) Dadan was not
  (3) often lied
  (4) Every night
  (5) garden

2 (1) ① Dadan's lessons
       ② the students work
  (2) ① D
       ② R
       ③ D
       ④ R
  (3) Yan will follow Rong-Wu because he is so talented and smiles gently (possible answer)

32 Reading Comprehension   pp 64,65

1 (1) ① dull
       ② hope
       ③ fear
       ④ confident
  (2) priceless
  (3) shook with fear
  (4) walk arm-in-arm

2 (1) nastier and nastier
  (2) to wiggle and fall
  (3) hundreds of paintings
  (4) his heart / his brush
  (5) No, Dadan was never seen again

33 Reading Comprehension   pp 66,67

1 (1) the opening in the hedge
  (2) a group of five tough-looking boys
  (3) to sound threatening
  (4) began to rummage inside it
  (5) the others / his friends

2 (1) dropped / the ground / put his foot
  (2) at the boy in disbelief
  (3) punishment / breaking the rules
  (4) Sixth-Grade Gate

34 Reading Comprehension   pp 68,69

1 (1) ① wimp
       ②③ creep, criminal
       ④ lunch-snatcher gang
       ⑤ new victims
  (2) ① backed
       ② the hedge
       ③ Sarah
       ④ spun
       ⑤ curly red
       ⑥ glasses

2 (1) stared at him in astonishment
  (2) feel powerful
  (3) late together
  (4) much better

35 Review
pp 70,71

1 (1) big / bigger / biggest

(2) happy / happier / happiest

(3) help / helpful / helpless

(4) careful / care / careless

(5) hungry / hungrily

2 (1) O

(2) S

(3) O

(4) S

(5) O

3 (1) petite

(2) refused

(3) unusual

(4) harvest

4 (1) to the lake's edge / a tree / look over the grasslands

(2) to come to him when he whistled

36 Review
pp 72,73

1 (1) whistled softly

(2) ©

2 (1) 3

(2) Carrots

(3) 2

(4) Fish

(5) 3

(6) oil

(7) 4

3 (1) ⓐ 5 ⓑ 6 ⓒ 1 ⓓ 4 ⓔ 2 ⓕ 3

(2) drive Maria to school / late for work

(3) her mother had made her favorite / ready to listen